Reunited

Iren

Series Edi

D0840679

WITHDRAWN

HEINLE
CENGAGE Learning™

Australia • Brazil • Japan • Korea • Mexico • Singapore • Spain • United Kingdom • United States

Page Turners Reading Library
Reunited
Irene Barrall

Publisher: Andrew Robinson

Executive Editor: Sean Bermingham

Senior Development Editor:
Derek Mackrell

Assistant Editors:
Claire Tan, Sarah Tan

Story Editor: Julian Thomlinson

Series Development Editor:
Sue Leather

Director of Global Marketing:
Ian Martin

Content Project Manager:
Tan Jin Hock

Print Buyer:
Susan Spencer

Layout Design and Illustrations:
Redbean Design Pte Ltd

Cover Illustration: Eric Foenander

Photo Credits:
93 Andrey Arkusha/Shutterstock

ISBN-13: 978-1-4240-1840-6

ISBN-10: 1-4240-1840-4

Heinle
20 Channel Center Street
Boston, Massachusetts 02210
USA

Cengage Learning is a leading provider of customized learning solutions with office locations around the globe, including Singapore, the United Kingdom, Australia, Mexico, Brazil, and Japan. Locate your local office at:
international.cengage.com/region

Cengage Learning products are represented in Canada by Nelson Education, Ltd.

Visit Heinle online at **elt.heinle.com**

Visit our corporate website at
www.cengage.com

Printed in the United States of America
2 3 4 5 6 7 – 14 13 12 11

Contents

People in the story

Ben and **Meg**

a young married couple

Jack
their two-year-old son

Gloria
Meg's friend

Laura Marsh
a writer from *Avant Garde
Magazine*

The story is set in New Hampshire, in the USA.

Chapter 1

Exciting news

Meg stood with her hands in her pockets, looking out of the studio window. The heater wasn't working, and she had a blanket over her shoulders to keep out the cold. The wind was coming up from the lake and blowing around the outside of the studio. She watched her husband, Ben, as he played in the garden with Jack, their two-year-old son. Father and son both wore ski jackets to keep out the cold. Jack laughed as Ben lifted him high in the air. Their brown-and-white dog ran over and jumped up, wanting to play.

Meg wanted to go out and join in the game. Instead she glanced over her shoulder at her unfinished painting. It was in the center of the studio, waiting for her. She knew she should get back to work, but still she stayed by the window. Her husband waved and carried their son in the direction of the lake. Meg smiled at her son's shouts of delight—he loved the water.

With a sigh, Meg turned and walked back to the painting. It was nearly finished, she knew, but she wasn't satisfied. The picture showed the covered bridge that Meg could see from her studio window. She looked out of the window at the river as it reflected the cold morning sky. Then she studied the painting again. It needed more white, she thought. Picking up her paintbrush, she started to paint.

The wooden bridges were famous in New Hampshire. Tourists came from all over the world to see them. Meg first got interested in them eight months earlier when she and

Ben moved to the area from New York. Now, most of her paintings were of the bridges in different seasons and different lights.

By the time she finished painting, it was almost one o'clock. She stood back and studied the picture. It wasn't perfect but it was certainly better. She washed the paint from her hands and was drying them when the telephone rang. Putting down the towel, she answered it.

"Meg, I've got some great news," announced the voice on the other end of the line.

"Hi, Gloria, what's got you so excited?" Meg asked, smiling at the sound of her friend's voice. Gloria was a cheerful forty-five-year-old who owned a gallery in town where Meg sold her paintings.

"You know *Avant Garde Magazine*?"

"*Avant Garde*? Isn't that an art magazine?"

"Not an art magazine, Meg, it's the art magazine—one of the most important in New York." Gloria didn't wait for Meg to reply before continuing breathlessly, "And they want to interview you."

"Me?" Meg's eyes were wide. "There must be some mistake."

"No, there's no mistake. They called me a minute ago."

"But why do they want to interview me?" Meg sat down on an old chair next to the window and brushed her dark hair back from her face.

"It's the most amazing luck. A writer from *Avant Garde Magazine* is interviewing local artists. One of the people she planned to interview is sick. So, she phoned the gallery and asked me to recommend another good artist in this area. I said that she should talk to you. She'll photograph some of your paintings for the article. Imagine what this could do for your sales!"

"Gloria. That's amazing!"

"She's coming to the gallery and then we'll drive to your studio, OK?"

"Sure, but when?"

"That's the problem." Meg could hear the hesitation in her friend's voice. "She's driving back to New York tonight. So she wants to see you at three o'clock this afternoon."

Meg looked down at the paint on her clothes.

"Three o'clock?" Meg looked around at the studio; there were books and drawings on the floor. "But I need to tidy. And what about Jack? How can I do an interview with a two-year-old running around?"

"Don't worry, I can look after Jack while you talk to the journalist." Gloria was businesslike. "Meg, this is a great opportunity for you as an artist. Are you really going to say 'no' to *Avant Garde Magazine*?"

Meg laughed. "OK, OK. I'll do the interview."

"Great. I'll call her now and arrange it. See you later."

"OK. Oh, Gloria, what's the writer's name?" She asked, but her friend had already gone.

Smiling to herself, she put down the phone, then ran over to the house to tell Ben the good news.

Chapter 2

A face from the past

Meg quickly showered and changed into her best green dress. Ben watched as she came down the stairs.

"You look great," he smiled.

She walked over and kissed him.

"So do you." She took a step back, pointing to the suit he had put on for his appointment with the bank. "Hey, we look like we're going on a date," she said.

"I wish we were. You're much prettier than the bank manager."

"But I can't give you lots of money to fix the roof," she said.

"That's true. But soon we won't need the bank. After the article appears in *Avant Garde Magazine*, everyone will want your paintings. You'll soon be rich and famous."

"And you'll only want me for my money," she kissed him again.

"Oh, I don't think so," he whispered.

She put her hand on his shoulder and looked into his face, suddenly uncertain. "Do you think they'll loan us the money, Ben?" she asked.

He smiled down at her, but she could see the worry in his eyes. "I sure hope so," he said.

She picked up Jack and walked with her husband to the car. The wind was colder now. She listened to it blow through the tops of the trees. Ben climbed into the truck, and they waved as he drove away along the track. As she turned back to the house, Meg glanced up at the roof. It was old and it would cost almost five thousand dollars to fix. She sighed and called to the dog, then she smiled at her son. "Come on," she said, "I'll make us a fire to keep warm."

After lunch she put Jack in his room for a nap, then she tidied the house. She looked at the clock nervously. It was almost time for the interview. Taking a brush, she looked in the mirror. Her green eyes suddenly looked too big in her pale face. She hesitated for a moment then pulled the brush through her brown hair, tying it back. Finally, she smoothed down her dress. It was simple and smart, the best thing she had. She remembered buying it when they lived in New York. How she had loved its lovely dark green color. Back then she could buy a new dress every month, sometimes every week. It seemed like another life—walking into shops and buying things you didn't really need or even want. But she was glad she had bought the green dress. Who knew how long it would be before she would be able to afford another?

Suddenly there was the sound of a car coming down the track. She put down the brush, recognizing the sound of Gloria's old car. Drops of rain hit the window as she looked out and watched Gloria park outside the house. A new sports car stopped behind it. A woman with short red hair got out of the second car. She was tall, wearing a stylish black coat and boots. Meg looked down at her green dress—she didn't feel smart anymore.

Taking a deep breath, Meg opened the door.

"We're late, sorry. It's like winter out here," Gloria apologized and hurried inside.

Meg watched as the other woman stepped into the warm house, brushing rain from her coat.

"This is Laura Marsh, from *Avant Garde Magazine*." Gloria said. "Laura, this is Meg."

Meg watched the woman run her fingers through her damp hair. There was something about the tall figure and the red-gold hair that made her stop.

"Laura Marsh?" Meg repeated the name quietly as she held out her hand. "I know that name. Have we met before?"

Laura shook her head, "I don't think so."

"You went to Dover College, didn't you? I did too. My name was Sears back then, Meg Sears."

A slow smile spread across Laura's face. "Of course, Meg Sears. Sorry, I didn't recognize you!"

"So you two know each other?" Gloria asked, confused.

"We were in the same year at college," Laura explained.

Meg remembered a quiet girl who wore gray sweaters and spent most of her time in the library. It was amazing to think she'd grown into this tall confident woman standing opposite her.

"Listen, I'll make us some coffee and you can tell me all about what you've been doing. I never get to see anyone from college. This is so great!"

Laura took a step to follow Meg into the kitchen. Suddenly, the dog got up from her place by the fire and walked over, making a low threatening noise. Laura stopped, her hands out in front of her.

"Keep that dog away from me."

Meg rushed over. "Bessy, stop it." She took the dog and put it outside. "Sorry, Laura. I don't know what's wrong with her."

"It's OK. I'm not very good with dogs." Laura's face was pale. "Look, Meg, I'm a little short on time. Could we leave the coffee and go and see your paintings?"

11

Chapter 3

Good-bye

In the studio, Laura made herself comfortable on the sofa, and Meg sat on a wooden chair opposite her. It was still cold, and rain spotted against the windows. Laura took out a notebook and ran through a few interview questions, making a note of Meg's answers. After a while she put down her notebook and pen.

"What?" Meg asked after a moment's silence. The other woman was watching her closely.

Laura smiled, "I was just thinking how amazing it is to meet you again like this. I always thought you were a city girl. What made you move here from New York?"

Meg hesitated before answering. "How did you know I lived in New York?" she said at last.

"I think Gloria said something," Laura replied, standing up and walking over to look at the paintings.

"Do you sell many?" she asked.

"Not enough. Mainly I sell through Gloria's gallery. She's great and she likes my work. Perhaps your article in *Avant Garde* will help us to sell more." Meg smiled.

Laura stopped in front of a large picture of a covered bridge. It was painted in blues and grays.

"This is really good. I can see why Gloria likes your paintings. When I asked her to recommend a good local artist for the article, yours was the second name she gave me."

"The second? Who did she recommend first?"

"Hmm? Oh, I can't remember. She said that the tourists like your pictures of the bridges."

"Not only tourists, I hope." Meg looked down at her hands. "Did Gloria say anything else?"

"What? No, not really. Anyway, the important thing is that you're a good artist."

"Thanks," said Meg, sounding less confident now. "So, how long have you been a writer?" she asked.

"About five years," Laura replied.

"Did you start writing after college?"

"Hey, who's doing the interviewing here?" Laura laughed.

At that moment, there was the sound of a truck outside.

"Come and meet Ben," Meg said, moving toward the door. Laura put her camera back in her bag, and they went outside.

As Ben got out of the truck, Meg knew immediately that something was wrong. The shadows under his eyes were even darker than when he had left that morning. He looked up and saw her, and his mouth opened to speak. But then he saw Laura and stopped.

"Ben, this is Laura from *Avant Garde Magazine*. We were at the same college. Laura, this is Ben."

"What a small world." Ben shook Laura's hand and tried to smile. "Well, let's get out of this cold. I'll make some coffee."

It was good to be in the warm house again. Gloria had already made coffee, and they sat by the fire. Jack sat next to Laura and played with her notebook.

Meg glanced around at her old furniture and wondered what Laura's place in the city looked like. She imagined a big, white apartment with modern paintings.

After a while, Gloria stood up. "I should get back to the gallery," she said, picking up her purse. "Don't forget, you said you'd work in the gallery on Monday," she reminded Meg. "You can bring your new painting over with you."

"It isn't finished yet," Meg said a little too quickly. After her conversation with Laura she felt unsure. Did Gloria really think her pictures were just for tourists?

Gloria turned to Laura. "I look forward to reading your article. Have a safe journey back to New York."

"I really should go too," Laura said, standing up. "I have a long drive."

"Why don't you stay to dinner?" Meg offered.

"I'd love to, but I have to go to a party to open a new art gallery in Manhattan."

"Hey, that sounds fun."

"It is, but it's tiring, too. I get a lot of invitations in this job, and it's always the same—lots of famous people who want ideas about which artist's work they should be buying. Sometimes I wish I could have a quiet evening at home."

"You should have a vacation here. We get lots of quiet evenings at home, don't we, Gloria?"

Gloria looked at her over her glasses, "Speak for yourself."

They walked with Laura to her sports car, Meg carrying Jack. After she got in, Laura opened the window.

"It was good to see you again, Meg. Here's my phone number. I hope we meet again soon."

They waved as she drove away down the track.

Chapter 4

An unexpected guest

Back in the warm kitchen, Ben and Meg looked at each other and let their social smiles slowly disappear.

"Were you pleased to meet up with your old college friend?" Ben asked.

"Yeah, it was a nice surprise, but it's not like we were big friends or anything. Anyway, our college days must seem pretty boring to her now she's a writer for a famous magazine."

"But did she like your paintings?"

"I'm not sure. I think maybe she saw me as a mom who paints for a hobby."

Ben came over and put his hand on her shoulder. "I'm sure she didn't think that. Anyone who sees your paintings can see that you're an artist."

She reached up and touched his face. "I don't need to ask how it went with the bank."

He sighed and sat at the kitchen table. Jack was eating his dinner and waving a piece of carrot in the air.

"They won't loan us any more money." Ben looked down at his hands. Meg had noticed how tired he looked these days.

"We'll find a way," she said quietly.

"How? We don't have any more savings and we need a new roof and windows." He stopped, shaking his head.

"But you only started your business a few months ago. Lots of people round here need help with their computers. You're getting more clients every month, you said so."

"Yes, but they don't pay enough." He ran his hand through his dark hair. "I wake up at night worrying about bills and payments. All I can see are numbers going round and round in my head, but none of the numbers add up. That's the problem.

"Don't worry, we'll get the money somehow."

"How? With your painting? Or perhaps Jack will find a magic money tree in the garden." He saw Meg's face and took her hand. "I'm sorry. I shouldn't say that. Your paintings are beautiful and I know you'll be a success. It's just we need money now. And it's all my fault."

"Your fault?"

"It's because of me that we left New York."

"Ben, don't. We did the right thing moving here." She got up and put her hand on his shoulder and he held it there for a moment.

The phone rang. She touched his hand and went to answer it.

"Hello? Meg?" Laura's voice sounded far away.

"Laura, what's happened?"

"There's a problem with the car. The engine stopped, and I can't get it started again. Do you think you or Ben could help me?"

"Of course. Do you have any idea where you are?"

"I'm at the end of the covered bridge, on the other side of the river."

"OK. Stay in the car. We'll be right there."

She put down the phone and looked at her husband. "Laura's car broke down. It looks like we have a guest for the night."

Ben stood up. "I'll go and get her."

"It's OK. I can do it." She reached for her coat.

"No, a drive will do me good." He kissed Meg and walked out into the dark.

By the time Laura and Ben got back, Meg had the dinner on and Jack was in bed. They came through the door laughing. Meg hurried over and took Laura's coat. She could smell beer as she went close to Ben.

"You were a long time," Meg said.

Laura and Ben exchanged glances. "That's my fault, Meg," she giggled. "I made Ben take me to a bar in town to warm me up before we came back here."

"I wish you'd phoned me, Ben. I was worried. So what happened with the car?"

Her husband shook his head, and rain fell from his curly hair. "I used the truck to bring it back here. I tried to call the mechanic, but he's out of town until tomorrow." Hearing Ben's voice, the dog got up from her place by the fire and walked over. Laura looked at the dog and moved away quickly.

"Don't worry. I'll take her for a walk and she can sleep outside tonight," Ben said. "You don't mind, do you, Bessy?" He touched the dog's head.

"Thank you." Laura smiled up at him.

"Well, I'll go and get your room ready," Meg said.

"I don't want to be any trouble," Laura said quickly. "I told Ben that I could stay at a hotel in town, but he wouldn't let me."

"No, don't be silly. It's great to have you here," Meg smiled.

When Meg came downstairs a little later, Laura was sitting on the sofa.

"Ben's still walking the dog," Laura said. "Look, I'm really sorry that we were so long with the car."

"Forget it. I was worried, that's all. It can get dangerous down by the river." Meg came over and took a seat beside Laura. "Do you ever see anyone from college?" she asked.

"No, do you?"

Meg shook her head. There were two or three people she exchanged Christmas cards with, but that was all.

"I think I have an old college yearbook somewhere. I'll get it out after dinner."

At that moment the door opened, and Ben came in. He brought with him the smell of damp leaves. But now Meg noticed another smell.

"Is something burning?" Ben asked, hanging his coat.

She rushed to the stove and opened the door. Smoke poured out.

"How did that happen?" She cried, burning her fingers as she tried to save the dinner. The chicken and potatoes were black. She dropped the dish onto the table.

"Hey, it's fine. I'll cook," Ben said.

There was a cry from upstairs.

"That's Jack" Laura said. "You go and see to him, and I'll help Ben with the dinner."

"There's steak in the refrigerator," Meg suggested, her voice tired.

"Don't worry. We have it all under control," Laura said as Meg went upstairs.

While she was getting Jack back to sleep, Meg could hear the sound of laughter and music downstairs. She came down to find the table prepared.

"This is all very nice," she said.

"Come and sit down," Laura smiled. For a moment Meg felt as though she were the visitor. Laura put the salad on the table, and Ben cut the bread

"I hope you don't mind omelette. I don't eat red meat," Laura explained. "I like simple things beautifully cooked. Oh I forgot . . ." She stood and went to the fridge, taking out a bottle and holding it up. "Champagne. I got it in town. I thought it was a good way to celebrate meeting again. Here's to reunited friends." Opening the bottle, she poured three glasses.

Meg and Ben raised their glasses. "To reunited friends," they said.

They began eating. "So, tell me what Meg was like at college," Ben asked Laura, smiling at his wife.

"When she arrived she became the most popular girl in college. It was amazing. She even started her own club."

"What sort of club was it?" Ben smiled.

"Oh it was too secret for people like you and me, Ben." Laura poured them each another glass of champagne. Meg put her hand over her glass. She was already getting a headache.

"It sounds much more exciting than it was," she said. "It was just a group of people who wanted to paint, or make films and videos. Mostly, we sat around and talked about where the next party would be."

"So, didn't you join, Laura?" Ben asked, offering her more salad.

"I was much too sensible, I spent all my time in the library. I didn't party at college, so I'm having my fun now."

Ben drank quickly and poured himself another glass. "I think you're doing the right thing. Not like us. Now it's all work and babies and money worries."

"Money worries?" Laura looked at Meg. "Nothing serious, I hope?"

"It's all fine," Meg said quickly. She gave her husband a warning look. Ben didn't seem to notice. "These old houses just eat money," he said.

"Ben, let's talk about something more interesting . . ."

"OK. So, Laura, were you surprised to find that Meg was a painter?"

"Not at all. At college we all thought Meg would be a famous artist," Laura said. "Everyone said she'd be a big star."

"And here I am, in an old house with a baby and paintings of bridges."

"Hey, that's not so bad is it?" Ben laughed, but there was worry in his eyes.

A little later, Ben stood up and stretched.

"I have to be up early tomorrow. So I'll clear the dishes and leave you two to talk about old times," he said.

Meg went over to a shelf and took down a red book. She pulled it out and took it to the sofa where Laura was sitting.

"Our old college yearbook," she said, holding it up. It had pictures of all the students from their time at Dover College.

Laura pulled a face, "Do we have to? I hate seeing myself in photos."

"Come on, it'll be fun." Meg turned the pages, pausing here and there when they saw a face that one of them recognized. At last they came to a full page photo of their year.

"There, that's you," Laura said, pointing to the center of the group. There was a younger Meg, laughing into the camera.

Meg looked closely, studying the faces.

"Where are you in the photo, Laura?" she asked.

Laura didn't answer for a moment; she waited in silence as Meg continued looking. At last, she pointed to a figure at the edge of the group—a girl with badly cut hair, watching the others without smiling. "That's me." She tapped the figure.

"Really? You've changed, Laura."

"Only on the outside," Laura replied, closing the book. "I really should go to bed, if that's OK, Meg. It's been a long day." She stood up.

"Oh, sure. Sorry. I should have realized." Meg looked up at her in surprise. Laura's face was half in the shadows, the other half reflecting the light from the fire. For a second, Meg could see the unsmiling, plain girl that Laura had been at college. Then a moment later it was gone.

After showing Laura to her room, Meg quietly opened the door to her bedroom. To her surprise, Ben was still awake. He sat up as she came in.

"Are you angry with me?" he asked quietly.

Meg sat in front of the mirror, and started brushing her hair.

"Of course not," she replied

"You seem a little tense," he continued, watching her.

Meg stopped brushing and turned to look at him.

"Well, why did you talk about money in front of Laura?" she asked.

"She's your old school friend, I didn't think . . ."

"No, you didn't think. She's not a friend, I haven't seen her in years. And what were you thinking taking her to a bar? You know how people in this town gossip."

"She just wanted to go for a drink, that's all. Why would people talk?"

"For the same reason they talked about you and Susan when you worked at Solmec? That was just a drink too, wasn't it?"

Ben's face went pale.

"I'm sorry, I must be tired. Forget I said that." Meg sighed and put down the brush.

"No, I can't because you'll never forget it, will you?"

"That's not true. When do I ever talk about it?"

"You don't have to— it's in your eyes. But if you need to hear it again, I'll repeat it. There was never anything between me and Susan. She was my boss, that's all."

"A boss who you went to lunch and dinner with so often that some kind person in your office thought they should write and tell me?"

"Shhh! You'll wake Jack and Laura." He spoke in an angry whisper. "The person who wrote that letter was trying to cause trouble. Alex wanted my job and he got it when I left the company. And the only reason I left was so that we could have a new start. When are you going to learn to trust me? I can't spend my life saying sorry for something I didn't do, Meg."

They stared at each other, eyes hot with anger. She turned and walked toward the door.

"Where are you going?" He asked

"I want to check that Jack's OK," she said, without looking at him.

"Meg, let's not do this. I don't want to fight." He tried to take her hand.

"I just want to be alone for a while." She moved away from him and went out, closing the bedroom door.

The hall was in darkness. Turning, she saw a shadow at the top of the stairs.

"Who's there?" she whispered, her heart beating fast. Suddenly the moon came out from behind a cloud. In its silver light, Laura stood like a statue watching her.

"Hey, you frightened me," Meg said, trying to smile.

"You're a nervous little thing, aren't you," Laura laughed quietly. "I was just getting some water." She held up a glass in her hand.

"Why didn't you turn the light on?" Meg asked. She realized her hands were shaking.

"I'm like a cat, I don't need light to find my way. See you in the morning, Meg."

"Yes, sleep well," Meg said.

Laura slowly walked back to her room. Before stepping inside, she turned back to Meg. "Sweet dreams," she said.

Chapter 5

A trip to town

The storm continued through the night. Meg found it hard to sleep. She lay in the darkness listening to the rain hit the windows. When she finally got to sleep, the first gray light was shining through the window. When she opened her eyes, the light was stronger and there were sounds from downstairs.

When she came down to the kitchen, Laura was already there looking fresh and relaxed. Meg looked at her and ran her fingers through her own untidy curls.

"You look tired. Here have this," Laura said, pouring a cup of coffee and giving it to her.

"Thanks. Jack woke me up," Meg lied.

There was already breakfast on the table. Ben saw her looking at it.

"Laura helped me make it. We didn't want to wake you," he explained.

His cell phone rang. He excused himself and took the call.

Laura was feeding Jack. He waved his hands happily at his mother and took another bite. Meg sat down and Laura handed her some toast.

"I cooked eggs. Would you like some?" she asked. Meg shook her head.

"No, I'm fine. You didn't need to do this, Laura."

"Don't be silly. I'm happy to help."

Ben returned to the table and quickly finished his coffee.

"That was Luke. He's got a problem with his computer. He wants me to go over this morning and take a look at it."

"On a Saturday?" Laura sounded surprised. "Don't you take weekends off?"

"When the work comes in, I have to take it. What have you two got planned today?"

"Well I guess we need to speak to the mechanic and arrange for him to look at Laura's car," Meg said.

"Oh, it's all arranged. I spoke to him this morning and he said he could look at it tomorrow."

"Tomorrow?"

"Yes," Laura looked from Meg to Ben. "I hope that's OK. I can move to a hotel if it's any problem."

"No, of course it's no problem," Meg said quickly. "But what about the party?"

"Party?" Laura stopped feeding Jack and looked at her.

"At the gallery in Manhattan?"

"Oh, do you know I almost forgot! I'll phone the owner of the gallery right away. These people get so angry if you miss their stupid parties without calling."

She handed Meg the spoon to feed Jack and disappeared upstairs with her cell phone.

Ben put on his jacket and checked that he had his keys. He kissed his son and Meg good-bye. Meg glanced at the stairs.

"Did she call our usual mechanic Jed?" she asked quietly.

"Sure, I gave her his number. She wanted to speak to him herself."

"And she said that she was staying with us?" She could hear Laura's steps in the room above.

"Yes, what's the problem?" Ben was looking at her.

"Nothing." Meg shook her head. "It's just usually Jed does the work the same day he's asked."

Ben looked at his watch. "Well, maybe he's busy this weekend like me. Look, do you want me to call him later and see if he can look at the car today?"

Meg hesitated; she could hear Laura's steps moving toward the stairs. "No, it's OK."

The door closed and there was the sound of his truck driving away. A sound made her look toward the stairs where Laura was watching her.

"All OK?" Meg asked.

"Yes, now why don't you show me around your little town?" Laura smiled.

Later that morning, they drove through the green countryside into town. Laura turned on the radio. For the first time Meg noticed her bitten fingernails. Everything else about Laura was so perfect that it was a surprise to see the red skin around her fingers. An old song came on, and Laura began singing quietly.

"Do you remember this song at college?"

"Oh yes," Meg pulled a face. "They always played it at the discos, didn't they?"

"I never went to the discos or the parties," Laura said. "But I remember seeing you and your friends sitting on the grass listening to it on the radio."

"When we probably should have been in the library doing work," Meg smiled.

"Oh, I spent a lot of time in the library. It looked like you and your friends were having a lot more fun."

Laura put her hands together and her bitten fingernails were hidden. She glanced at Meg quickly, suddenly looking very young. "You know, I never told you this, but I really admired you at college."

"Me? Why?" Meg felt a mix of embarrassment and pleasure.

"Oh, I don't know. You always seemed to be at the center of things; you were the leader and not a follower." Meg turned onto the main road and drove past the lake toward the river.

"Well, that's a very nice thing to say. But really, I was just one of the group." She smiled, enjoying the picture of herself as a leader. It seemed such a long time ago that she had been young and confident and free from worry.

"No, that's not true. Like that club you started, remember? Everyone wanted to be a part of it. It must have been exciting."

Meg laughed and shook her head; a brown curl fell over her eye. "No, like I said last night. We just sat around talking. We didn't really do a lot."

"But there were some interesting people in your group, Doug Martin, for example. Didn't you date him for a while?" Laura looked down at her red fingernails.

"Doug Martin? Yeah. Did you know him? Oh, wait, I remember, you two were friends, weren't you?" Meg nodded slowly. She had a sudden memory of a tall boy with blond hair—Doug Martin. She hadn't thought of him in years.

"For a while. Do you remember he played guitar in that band?"

"Yeah, they were really bad. We only dated for a few weeks, but he was a nice guy. Do you still see him?"

"Oh, no, not since college."

"The only problem was he liked to play jokes. He used to phone me and pretend to be a teacher, that kind of thing. It got a little boring."

"He always tried to be funny around cool people. I guess he wanted people to like him." There was something in Laura's voice that made Meg look at her.

They were almost at the river. The road went through a long covered bridge that connected the towns of Windsor and Cornish.

"This is the longest covered bridge in the USA," Meg pointed out, suddenly glad to be able to change the subject. The river was high from the previous night's rain.

When they arrived in town, Meg parked the car. As they walked across the town square, she pointed out the places of interest. Laura looked around her.

"Forget the sightseeing; show me the stores!" she said.

Meg laughed and relaxed. "I thought you'd want to go to the museum. Weren't you in the history club at college?"

"That's because it was the only club that invited me. Come on, let's go and enjoy ourselves!"

They started at Luella's boutique where Laura bought a new purse. Then she bought a dress and a pair of boots. Later, she bought them lunch at the restaurant. Meg tried to remember the last time she spent a morning clothes shopping. She had forgotten how enjoyable it could be.

"I'm really glad your car broke down or we wouldn't have had this chance to get to know each other," Meg said.

"Me too. Back at college I never imagined that Laura Marsh and Meg Sears would end up having lunch together." Laura pushed away her plate; she had hardly touched her food.

Chapter 6

The lake

When they got back to the house, Laura announced that she wanted to go for a walk. Meg looked down at Jack; it was already past the time for his nap. Laura put her hand on her arm.

"Don't worry. I can go on my own. I won't get lost, I promise," she said.

Meg took Jack to his room. But he cried and didn't want to be left alone. He held his old toy rabbit in one hand.

"Do you want to come into Mommy's bed for a while?" she asked.

They went into Meg's room and lay on the bed. Jack soon fell asleep. She watched his chest rising and falling. Putting her arm over her son, she closed her eyes and listened to the wind outside the window.

When she woke Ben was standing by the bed.

"Hi there. I just got back," he said quietly. "You must have been tired."

She sat up and stretched. The warm feeling that stayed with her from her dream was replaced by fear. She brushed her hair from her eyes and looked around her.

"Where's Jack?"

"Jack? Isn't he in his own bed?" Ben said.

She shook her head, her heart beating quickly. "No, he was here with me. I must have fallen asleep."

"Where's Laura? Maybe he's with her?" Ben was trying to keep his voice calm.

"She went for a walk." Meg stood up and put her hand to her mouth, her eyes wide "Where can he be?"

"Don't worry, we'll find him." Ben checked Jack's room again, while Meg hurried downstairs.

Outside everything was unnaturally quiet. Suddenly, she heard a cry. She looked around wildly; where was the sound coming from? The cry came again from the direction of the lake. Turning, she saw a small figure in the water.

Jack.

She ran, her heart beating fast. It was like some terrible dream where she ran and ran and yet got no closer to the tiny figure in the water. Her chest was on fire, every breath painful.

Suddenly, Laura appeared at the bottom of the hill, close to the lake. Without hesitating, she ran in and lifted Jack from the water. Meg ran across the grass, crying.

"What happened? What did you do to him?" She pulled her son away from Laura and held him close to her chest.

"Meg, I know you're upset, but you need to put Jack on the grass. We need to check that he's OK." Meg ignored her and held her son tightly. After a moment's horrible silence, Jack's cry filled the air.

"It's OK, baby. Mommy's here." Meg kissed his head.

Ben ran up to them. He took off his jacket and wrapped it around his son. Jack had stopped crying and was looking with interest from his mother to his father.

"Wet," he said, pointing to something on the ground. Meg looked down and saw her son's rabbit at the edge of the pond. She picked it up, looking at it. Jack never took the rabbit out of the house. He was always frightened of losing it. Why would he bring it down to the lake?

Back at the house, she warmed Jack in the bath. She dried him and put dry clothes on him and then took him downstairs. Meg tried to give him his rabbit but he shook his head.

"Bad rabbit," was all he said. Ben took his son to sit by the fire and read him a story while Meg went to the kitchen to make them hot chocolate.

Laura was sitting at the kitchen table.

"Do you want hot chocolate?" Meg asked, without looking at her.

"No thanks. Look, have I done something wrong?"

Meg wouldn't meet the other woman's eye. She opened cupboard doors and took out cups.

"Meg, speak to me." Laura got up.

"What was he doing outside?" Meg asked angrily, turning to look at her friend for the first time. "How did he get out?"

"I don't know. I wasn't here. I was out walking. You were the one that was here, Meg."

"What are you saying?"

"I'm not saying anything. I'm trying to find out why you're so angry with me. What did I do?"

"Did you take my son down to the lake?" Meg demanded. She realized she was shouting but she couldn't stop herself. Waving her arm, she hit a cup, and it fell to the floor and broke.

"What's going on here? You're frightening Jack."

They turned to see Ben standing at the door. He walked over to his wife and put his hand on her arm.

"Meg, I understand that you're upset; we all are. But it was Laura who saved Jack. You saw her."

Meg put her hands over her face, breathing in and out.

"Laura, I'm so sorry," she said at last. She started to cry quietly. "I was so angry with myself for letting this happen."

"I understand," Laura said. She walked over and put her hand on Meg's shoulder. Meg reached up and took her hand.

The next morning Laura was playing in the garden with Jack. They looked like a strange pair, Laura in her elegant pantsuit and Jack in his Spiderman suit. Meg watched them though the window. An anxious feeling remained in her stomach. Probably shock and too much coffee, she told herself. She hadn't slept well again either.

Ben came and stood behind her. She still couldn't talk to him about the accident at the lake. Every time she tried, the words wouldn't come out. But she worried that he blamed her. It wasn't anything that he said. But he made sure that he was around to watch Jack, as though he was frightened it could happen again.

There was the sound of a truck coming down the drive. Meg went to the door in time to see Jed the mechanic getting out. She introduced him to Laura and they walked over to the sports car.

"Hey, nice car," Jed said.

"At the moment, I just want a car that works," Laura said.

"I was in this area yesterday afternoon. I could've come over then." Jed leaned over and looked at the engine.

"Laura thought you were busy yesterday, Jed," Meg said.

"No, yesterday was real quiet. I thought you were all out for the day."

"Shall we make Jed a coffee while he takes a look at the car?" Laura asked, walking toward the house.

When they were in the kitchen, Laura ran her hand through her hair. "Sorry for any confusion," she said. "I'm afraid I found it a little difficult to understand what Jed was saying on the phone. I should have let you or Ben make the call."

"Don't worry about it. The important thing is that Jed can fix your car."

When they brought out the coffee, Ben was standing by the car talking to Jed.

"It's all fixed," Ben said.

"Wow, that was quick," Meg said, handing the cup of hot coffee to Jed.

"It was no problem." Jed pointed to the engine. "This part here had come out. Did you say it happened when you were driving along?" he asked Laura.

"That's right. How much do I owe you?"

Jed shook his head. "No, it's OK. Ben here already paid. Well that's a strange one. I never saw it come out when the car's driving along."

"Well there's a first time for everything," Laura said. "Thanks again." She turned and started to walk back to the house.

Jed was still looking at the car, "You sure you were driving when it happened. You didn't stop first?"

Laura turned back. "Yes, of course I'm sure."

"Perhaps you stopped for a moment?" Meg suggested. The conversation was suddenly tense and she didn't know why.

"I told you," Laura said slowly, "I was driving through the covered bridge and when I got to the other side of the river, the engine stopped."

"OK. If you say so, lady." Jed took off his hat and put it back on again. "Well, thanks for the coffee, Meg." He paused as he passed Laura. "You should take that car to a garage when you get back to New York."

"I will," Laura smiled. "Thanks again for your help."

Laura lifted Jack as they watched the mechanic's truck leave. "What a funny little man," Laura said and Jack laughed.

When they went back to the house, Laura went upstairs to her room.

"What did Jed say about the car?" she asked Ben.

"You know what Jed's like. It's difficult to get him to say exactly what he means. He said the last time he'd seen something like this, the owner had pulled out a wire in the engine by mistake."

"Does he think Laura did that?" Meg asked.

"No, he didn't say that." Ben put his hand on her shoulder. "You know Jed, he's more comfortable fixing trucks not sports cars. Anyway, the most important thing is the car is fixed and it'll get Laura home." He glanced at the stairs and moved closer to Meg, "Do you think she'll leave today?" he asked quietly.

Meg glanced at the stairs too. "I don't know. She saved Jack, so I can't ask her to go to a hotel, can I?"

"No, of course not. It's nice that you have a friend to stay." Ben leaned forward to kiss her.

"Anyway," Meg said, moving away, "you seem to like having her here."

He stopped and turned to her. "She's your friend, Meg. I'm trying to make her welcome, that's all," he said.

"Well it seems you made her so welcome she wants to stay."

"What do you mean?" His voice was louder now.

"You know what I mean."

"I don't believe this." Ben shook his head glaring at her. "Don't you realize how important trust is? I only want you Meg. I have only ever wanted you."

She didn't answer. He watched her back tense as she cleared away the breakfast things.

"Look, if you want to know her plans, why don't you just ask her?" Ben said, walking away.

"Ask her what?"

Meg jumped and turned to see Laura standing at the bottom of the stairs.

"Meg, you really need to take something for your nerves," Laura smiled. "Now what did you want to ask?"

Meg could feel her face getting red and hot.

"We were saying that you must be pleased that the car is fixed, because now you can get back to work tomorrow."

"Actually, I was thinking, I've got some vacation time and I thought I might ask if I could stay on a few more days. It's so lovely around here."

"Stay?" Meg glanced across at Ben but he looked away. "Sure. I just thought you needed to get back to New York to write the article."

"No, I don't need to finish that until next month. So there's no need to rush back." She looked from Ben to Meg. "Are you sure it would be OK?"

"Of course," Meg said quickly.

"You won't even know that I'm here, I promise. Now, you must let me take you to lunch to say thank you. Go and get Jack and we'll go to the best restaurant in town."

Just before they left, Ben went outside and called the dog. After a moment, he came back in.

"Meg, have you seen Bessy this morning?"

"No, and look, she hasn't eaten the food I put out for her this morning."

"Don't worry," Laura said. "I'm sure she'll be here when we get back from lunch."

Meg stayed at the door calling the dog. Laura picked up her coat and walked toward the door. "Come on, Jack's hungry," she called.

After a moment's hesitation, Meg turned and followed her to the car.

Chapter 7

Where's Bessy?

Meg was quiet in the restaurant. She glanced nervously at the glasses on the table. Jack was sure to knock over his drink or break something. She wished they were in their usual restaurant in town where they could relax. But Laura had wanted to go somewhere special, and Ben was happy to show her that Cornish could serve food as good as anywhere in New York City. When they first sat down at the table, the only person talking was Laura. Meg looked at Ben once or twice, but she could see that he was still angry with her. Instead she made sure that Jack was okay. He was the only child in the place. Now Laura was talking to Ben about his computer business. She listened to his answers carefully, nodding in agreement. Meg realized with sadness that more and more of her own conversations with Ben seemed to be about money or problems with the house. They rarely got to talk about what they were thinking or feeling.

Jack was sitting on the seat, playing with a red toy car. He turned to look out of the window. There was a small garden with flowers.

"Would you like me to take you out there so that you can play with your car?" Meg asked.

He looked out the window again and nodded.

It was cold, but it was good to feel the wind in her hair. Jack was happier, too. He ran from one side of the garden to the other pretending to be a plane. Meg wore her jacket over her shoulders. Through the window she could see Laura and Ben talking. Laura laughed at something Ben said, and Meg noticed that she never took her eyes from his face—like someone on a date. The thought made her uncomfortable.

"Jack, come on. It's time we went back in," she called.

When they arrived back at the house, Ben went outside to check on Bessy. When he returned, he looked worried.

"She's not there and she still hasn't eaten her food," he said.

"Maybe she ran off," Laura said.

"No, she likes to go over to the fields, but she always comes back."

Meg looked at the gray sky. There was still over an hour of daylight left.

"I'll go look for her. You stay here with Jack."

"I'll help you," Laura offered, reaching for her coat.

But Meg shook her head. "I'll take the bike, I won't be long."

She felt the rain against her face as she hurried to the barn where she kept her motorbike. She went down the farm track, mud flying behind her. Even with her heavy jacket, she could feel the cold wind rushing past the bike.

First, she checked the places where she and Ben walked the dog, but Bessy wasn't there. Next, she tried the forest. She knew the dog liked to go there to try and find rabbits. It was almost dark. Sadly, she turned the bike around to head for home. Then she looked up and saw the small building in the distance. It was on the edge of their land, but they never used it. It was very old, and the roof and windows had holes. She looked at the sky again and then decided to have a quick look before setting off for home.

She heard Bessy before she saw her. At first she thought it was the wind. But then she heard it again. The door to the building was closed, a rock in front of it. She moved the rock and opened the door. Taking out her flashlight, she turned it on and shone the yellow light into the shadows. Bessy was in the corner. When she saw Meg she tried to get up, but she was too weak. She lifted her head and her tail moved once, but then she lowered her head again and closed her eyes.

Meg phoned Ben on her cell phone. When he arrived, together they gently lifted the dog into the back of the truck and took her back to the house. Meg raced ahead on her motorbike and called the veterinarian. By the time he arrived, Bessy was much worse. She couldn't lift her head and she was making noises as though she was in a lot of pain.

After checking Bessy over, he washed his hands and shook his head.

"If you hadn't found her tonight, it would have been too late," he said.

"But what made her so ill?" Meg asked. Bessy had finally fallen asleep in front of the fire, a blanket over her. Every now and then she made little noises in her sleep.

"She might have eaten something bad. Do you know if any of your neighbors use poison to kill rats?" he asked.

"None of the farms around here uses poison," Ben said. "We all have dogs and kids."

"Will she be OK?" Meg asked anxiously.

The veterinarian packed his bag before replying. He was a short man with white hair and glasses. Every word and action was slow and careful.

"I can't say for sure, but she's a strong dog."

Ben walked the veterinarian to his truck. Laura sat with the kitchen table between herself and Bessy.

"It's amazing you found him," she said.

"Her," Meg corrected. "Yes, it is. I still don't know what she was doing down there. She could have died."

"That's why I don't have an animal. Too much trouble," Laura said.

Chapter 8

An accident at the gallery

Monday morning started out bad and got worse. Ben was talking to Meg only when necessary. She wanted to put her arms around him and make it stop, but as time went on she became angry with him, too. They spoke to each other politely but didn't use more words than necessary. So when he finished his breakfast and stood up to put on his coat, Meg said simply.

"Where are you going?"

He kissed his son's head and looked across the table at his wife.

"I have a job to do in a company over in Hamilton. They're having computer problems." He picked up his keys and started walking toward the door.

"But I'm working in the gallery this morning. I told you!"

"Oh, I forgot. Look, you can take Jack to the gallery with you. I need to do this job; they pay well and they might have a lot more work for me." The shadows under his eyes were darker this morning.

"Ben, I can't take Jack, Gloria has some new glass statues in the gallery. At the moment, it's too dangerous to have a two-year-old running around in there."

"Well, phone Gloria and cancel, she'll understand." Ben moved his keys from hand to hand.

"No! It's not my mistake, it's yours." There was a cold edge to Meg's voice.

They faced each other angrily over the kitchen table.

"It's not a problem," Laura said, pouring coffee. "I can go into town with you and Jack, and we can go to the park while you work in the gallery."

"Are you sure? Thanks, Laura, that's a real help," Meg said.

"No problem, I'm happy to help," Laura smiled.

They finished breakfast quickly and drove into town. When they got to the gallery, Gloria was waiting.

"I'm glad you got here. I don't want to be late," she said to Meg smiling. Then she turned to the other woman. "Laura, this is a surprise! I thought you would be back in New York by now!"

"It's so lovely here, it's hard to leave." Laura took off her coat and looked around the gallery. She walked over to a table of glass figures and picked one up.

"How long are you planning to stay?"

Meg tried not to smile. One of the things that she loved about Gloria was her direct way of asking questions.

"I'm not sure." Laura put down the glass figure. "But it's lucky for Meg that I was here today."

"Is that right?" Gloria turned to Meg. "Why's that?"

"Just a little communication problem," Meg said, putting Jack on the floor while she took off her coat. He immediately ran over to the table, attracted by the light reflecting off the glass figures.

Gloria took a step forward and stopped him. "Careful, Jack." She looked across at Meg. "He isn't staying with you today is he, Meg? It's too dangerous with all this glass."

"It's OK. Jack and I are going to the park and then to the shops," Laura said.

"Laura's being a real help," Meg smiled.

"I can see she is," Gloria nodded, watching Laura. "OK, I'll be back at midday. Oh, I forgot. I'm expecting a delivery. Can you pay the guy? There's a lot of cash in my desk in the office."

"Gloria, did you forget to go to the bank again?" Meg shook her head.

"I was busy," Gloria explained. "I'll go as soon as I get back from my appointment, I promise."

With a wave she left, hurrying across the town square.

"I hope Gloria doesn't make a habit of leaving cash around. It's dangerous."

"I know, that's what I tell Gloria all the time. She forgets to go to the bank and then you look in her desk and there's thousands of dollars. But don't worry. It's very safe here in Cornish. I'll remind Gloria when she gets back."

"Do you work here often?" Laura asked. She saw one of Meg's paintings near the window and went to study it.

"Two or three times a week. It helps Gloria when she needs to go out."

"And I guess the money helps you, too." Laura was still studying the painting and didn't notice Meg go red. "Come on, Jack, let's go find the park and have some fun."

Meg gave them directions and watched them leave. She began arranging art books on a small round table. What Laura had said had made her think. Had Gloria started to ask her to help at the gallery just because she knew they needed the money? The thought made her feel uncomfortable. She walked to the glass figures and picked up a price list. They were four hundred dollars each. She was certainly glad that she didn't need to worry about Jack touching them.

The morning passed slowly. It was after midday when Laura and Jack arrived back. Jack's face was pink with cold and excitement. They were both laughing as they hurried in, bringing with them the smell of fall leaves.

"Look! Rain!" he held up a large red train in his arms.

"Did Laura buy you that?" Meg looked at the train trying to keep the disappointment from her voice.

"Yes, I hope it's OK. We went into a shop to get out of the rain and he really wanted it," Laura said, looking at Meg.

Meg knew how much her son wanted the train. He pointed to it every time they passed the shop window. She and Ben had saved to buy it for his third birthday next month. Hadn't she mentioned that to Laura the last time they came to town? Perhaps she was mistaken.

"It's very kind of you, Laura," she said quickly. "I hope Jack was a good boy."

"Oh we had a great time, didn't we, Jack?"

He ignored her, playing with his train on the floor. Meg took their wet coats. "I'll put these near the heater in the office to dry. Do you want a coffee?" she asked.

"That'd be great, and a towel, too, if Gloria has one." Laura ran her fingers though her wet hair.

Meg was walking back toward the main gallery when she heard the crash. Rushing into the gallery, she put the tray of coffee on the table. "What's happened?" she called. But she didn't need a reply; she could see for herself. Jack was sitting on the floor, eyes wide. Around him lay pieces of broken glass figures. Laura was near him, trying to keep him away from the glass. She glanced up. "Meg, I'm so sorry. I only took my eyes off him for a second. He must have crashed the train into the table."

"Careful, Jack!!" Meg rushed over and picked up her son. She looked down at the broken figures in horror.

"You look after Jack. I'll get something to put the broken figures in." Laura rushed out. A little later, she returned with a small box and put in the broken figures, three in total. Meg's closed her eyes in horror at the thought of how close Jack had come to getting hurt. She carried her son away from the table. How much had Gloria said the figures cost—four hundred dollars each? That was more than a thousand dollars worth of broken glass. Meg bit her lip. What was she going to say to her friend?

Chapter 9

Fire!

Ten minutes later, the bell on the shop door rang. Gloria hurried in and nodded hello to Meg. She brushed rain from her coat.

"Sorry I'm late," she said breathlessly. She glanced up and saw Laura, holding Jack. "Oh, hi, you're back. Did you have fun at the park? Hey, what's wrong?"

Without saying anything, Meg and Laura glanced at the display table. She followed their gaze. Whatever she had been about to say was forgotten. Gloria rushed over to the table, her hand over her mouth as she looked at the destroyed display. The three broken figures lay in the box. "How did this happen?" she asked at last.

"Jack had a little accident," Laura said quietly.

"Gloria, I'm so sorry. I don't know how . . ."

Before Meg could finish, Gloria interrupted, "Is Jack OK?" she asked.

"Yes, he's fine, thanks. I was only out of the room for a moment," Meg said.

Jack was playing quietly with his train. He held it up for Gloria to see. She put her hand on his head.

"I'm just glad he's not hurt," she said, but she still sounded upset. She looked around the room. "Is something burning?" she asked, walking quickly to the back of the gallery. Meg followed, watching as Gloria stepped carefully over the pool of coffee on the floor. The smell of burning was much stronger here. Gloria opened the office door. They covered their ears as a fire alarm started to ring nearby. Smoke poured out of the office.

"Let's get out of here," Gloria ordered, quickly closing the office door.

Running back to the main gallery, Meg picked up Jack, and the three women hurried outside. Gloria called 911 on her cell phone and quickly explained the situation. Across the street, Meg saw a familiar figure. It was Vince Harper, the sheriff.

"Sheriff, we need help over here," she called.

When Meg explained what had happened, he ran inside the gallery. The three women waited anxiously outside in the cold. In the distance, Meg could hear the sound of the fire truck getting closer. She held Jack gently as he started to cry.

Half an hour later they sat together inside the gallery, all the doors and windows open. The smoke had gone, but there was an unpleasant smell of burning. Jack waved to the firefighters as they walked past carrying equipment. He ran over and grabbed his red train holding it up proudly for them to see. The sheriff was talking quietly to the fire chief in the corner. After a moment, he came over and nodded to the women.

"Well, it seems that the fire started because some coats had been put on top of a heater," he said.

"What?" Gloria was saying, shaking her head again. "Meg, I told you so many times not to put things on the heaters."

Meg leaned forward. "Gloria, I promise you that I didn't put any coats on the heater. I put them over a chair near it so they could dry. Laura and Jack got wet in the rain."

The sheriff held a cup of coffee in his big hands. "Perhaps they fell onto the heater?" he suggested. "Laura says there was an accident with the glass. Maybe you were hurrying

and . . ." He looked down at his coffee without finishing the sentence.

"No, it wasn't like that," Meg said. Her eyes hurt from the smoke, and she wiped them with the back of her hand.

"Well, the good news is that there isn't much damage. A few minutes later, the fire would have spread, and then you could have lost the whole gallery."

"I'll go in and take a look." Gloria got up. She looked tired, and her eyes were red.

"I can't let you do that." The sheriff stood in front of her, blocking her way. "We can't let anyone in there at the moment. If there's anything you need, tell me and I'll get it for you."

Gloria put her hand to her head and thought for a moment. "There's money in my desk. I didn't have time to go to the bank yesterday."

"OK, I'll get it for you. How much is there?"

"Five thousand dollars," Gloria replied.

"Five thousand!" The sheriff looked like he was about to give her a talk about leaving that kind of money in her office, but he saw her face and stopped.

"Like I said I didn't get to the bank and I had a big delivery coming today. Did it arrive, Meg?"

Meg shook her head, trying not to notice the coldness in her friend's voice when she said her name.

They sat in silence while the sheriff went to the office. Meg noticed that Gloria wouldn't meet her eye.

"I'm hungry, Mommy," Jack said. He began playing with his hair the way he always did when he was tired.

"We'll go home soon and I'll make you some lunch," Meg

promised, trying to smile. "Gloria, would you like to come home with us?"

Her friend shook her head. "No, I just want to go home and have a shower."

For a moment, Meg had forgotten that Laura was there. Then she heard her voice behind her chair.

"Gloria, will you let me come back with you? I can make you some lunch and make sure you're OK. This has been a terrible shock; you need someone to look after you."

Meg felt a wave of anger at Laura and immediately felt bad. She was only offering to help, after all.

Before Meg could reply, the sheriff came back.

"Gloria, are you sure that the money was in your office?" he asked.

She looked up. "It's in my desk. What's wrong?"

The sheriff shook his head. "Maybe I didn't look in the right place. Wait a minute and I'll check." He went off. The three women looked at each other in confusion. Gloria looked like she might cry any moment.

"Gloria, I'm so sorry . . ." Meg was interrupted by the sheriff's return. His mouth was closed in a tight line. When he spoke there was an official ring to his voice.

"I found it, but there's only two thousand here," he said. Gloria's face was white.

"There was five thousand when I left this morning." She stood up as though she was about to go into the office. The sheriff blocked her way again.

"I really can't let you do that. Gloria, I looked all over. This is all the money in the office, believe me."

"Then where is it? Tell me that." Gloria was crying now.

She wiped her eyes and glared at them. "Where is it?" she repeated, louder this time.

"Did you have any customers this morning?" he asked Meg. She shook her head.

"And you two were here together?" he asked Laura.

"Well, we arrived together; then I took Jack out. We were a little late back; we got here just before Gloria."

Meg's heart started to beat faster as the sheriff's attention turned to her again. "And no one else came in? You're sure the delivery man didn't come?"

Meg shook her head again.

"No, it was quiet all morning." She could feel her hands starting to shake.

"Look, I'm sure there's a very simple explanation. Let's start by going though pockets and bags. Does anyone have a problem with that?" the sheriff asked.

The three women shook their heads. Each one emptied her pockets and put the items on the table.

"OK, now let's take a quick look at your purses." The sheriff looked a little uncomfortable as they got their purses and returned to the table. Gloria went first. Her bag was filled with tissues and candy and perfume. Laura's had only an expensive wallet and keys. Meg put her own purse on the table and took out the items one by one: a toy car, a small notebook, a pen, her old wallet, one of Jack's drawings.

"That everything?" the sheriff asked, looking more relaxed. She nodded. That was everything she had put in her bag this morning, she was sure. She put her hand in for a final check. She looked up in shock. At the bottom of the bag, her hand rested on something made of paper.

"What is it, Meg?" Laura asked, seeing her face.

She took out the paper. A tight roll of green bills. She dropped it onto the table as though it had burned her fingers.

"Is that money yours?" the sheriff asked. He was already getting out his notebook. Meg looked from him to Gloria.

"No, it's not. I don't know how it got there!"

Gloria was staring at the cash as though she couldn't believe what it was.

"Maybe we should talk about this down at the station," the sheriff said quietly.

She looked from the sheriff to the two women in horror. When she finally spoke, her voice sounded strange to her own ears. "What about Jack?" she asked.

The sheriff looked down at her son. "Jack will be just fine with Gloria and Laura. They can contact Ben. This won't take too long."

Laura put her hand on Meg's shoulder. "Don't worry, I'll look after him." She turned to the sheriff. "This is a terrible mistake; Meg hasn't done anything wrong."

Meg looked at her with a blank expression. It all seemed like a horrible dream.

But as the sheriff put his hand on her arm and led her out of the gallery, she knew she wasn't about to wake up.

When they reached the door, Meg suddenly turned round and looked at Laura, staring into the other woman's eyes. For a moment Meg looked as though she was about to speak. But instead she turned and followed the sheriff to his car.

Chapter 10

The missing watch

It was dark when she got home. The house lights shone out across the yard. Through the window she could see Laura talking to Ben and feeding Jack. It looked like the perfect family scene. She hesitated before going inside, feeling like a stranger in her own home.

Earlier, she had phoned Ben while she was at the station. She explained that she wanted him to collect Jack and go home.

"But I want to be with you." She could hear the worry in his voice.

"Jack needs you more. I don't want him to be frightened."

"If that's really what you want, Meg," he said quietly. Down the phone line she could hear the distance between them.

Now she was back in her own yard. She wasn't sure how long she stood outside, looking through the window. Suddenly the door opened.

"Meg, is that you?" Ben called, his worried face looking out into the darkness. Meg stepped into the circle of light and let him take her in his arms. Feeling his familiar warmth, she relaxed a little. "Come inside," he brought her in and she sat by the fire. Jack carried the red train over to her and gave it to her.

"Is that for me?" she asked. Her son nodded and jumped onto the sofa next to her, throwing his arms around her neck. Bessy hurried over and put her head on Meg's leg. Ben sat on the arm of the sofa.

"Tell us what happened at the station."

Meg shook her head; she didn't really know herself. "They asked a lot of questions that I had no answers to. Gloria left the sheriff a message to say it was a mistake, that she put the money in my bag by accident and then forgot. It took a long time, but finally they let me go." She looked at the fire. How long had she been at the station? No more than two hours, yet it seemed like days.

"But I know Gloria lied to the police when she said that she put the money in my bag," she said.

"Well, you did say that she often forgot things."

Meg turned to see Laura standing at the edge of the group.

"Yes, but not something as important as this. No, she said that she put the money in my bag so that the police would let me go. I'll phone her." She started to get up.

"Gloria isn't at her house. She went to stay with her sister this afternoon," Laura said.

Meg looked at Ben and he nodded. "That's right. She left just before I arrived," Ben said.

"It's OK. I'll call her cell phone." But after a moment, Meg put down the phone. "That's strange, she isn't answering. She usually keeps her phone on all the time. Did she leave a number at her sister's?"

Laura shook her head. "Not with me. Now, why don't you go and have a hot bath while I put Jack to bed? Then I'll make us some dinner."

Meg couldn't remember the last time she had felt so tired. The thought of sitting in a nice hot bath was wonderful. But she shook her head and stood up, shaking off the feeling that she was still in a dream.

"Thanks for the offer, Laura, but no."

The other woman took a step toward her. "You've had a shock. You need to rest."

Meg didn't reply. Instead she picked up her son. "Ben, could you put Jack to bed? There's something I need to do." Ben looked at Meg with a question in his eye, but he did as she asked and took his son upstairs.

She could feel Laura staring at her as she walked over to the refrigerator and opened the door.

"What is it, Meg? Do you want something to eat? Let me fix something for you," Laura offered, stepping forward.

"No, I'm fine." Meg closed the refrigerator door. "I need to get some air. I won't be long." Before the other woman could offer to go with her, Meg grabbed her coat and hurried outside. A moment later there was the sound of her motorbike engine as she raced across the fields.

She returned to the house half an hour later. Ben was waiting with Laura in the kitchen. Meg could see the worry on his face when she came in.

"Meg, where have you been?" he asked.

"It's OK, Ben. I went for a ride across the fields."

"But it's dark and cold. Are you OK, Meg?" He stepped forward and looked into her face. She smiled and put her hand on his face.

"Yes, I'm fine, Ben." She took off her coat and noticed Laura watching her closely.

"Are you sure you don't want to rest, Meg?" Laura exchanged glances with Ben.

"Perhaps Laura's right," Ben said. "Why don't you lie down and I'll bring you something to eat."

"No I don't need to rest." Meg walked over to the table and sat down. "But you're right, I am hungry. Laura, would you be able to get me something to eat?"

"I'll do it," Ben said.

"No, that's very kind of you, darling." Meg put her hand on her husband's to keep him near her. "Laura is such a wonderful cook. You don't mind, do you?" she said, smiling at the other woman.

"Of course not," Laura said brightly, walking toward the refrigerator. "Now, what would you like?

Meg was quiet for a moment, thinking.

"What I'd really like is a nice big steak," she said at last. Laura stood with her back to her. Meg could see the other woman's shoulders tense. She opened the refrigerator, its yellow light reflecting against her skin.

"You don't have any steak in here. Can I make you something else?" Laura asked.

"I'm sure there's steak in there. Did you eat it, Ben?"

Ben looked at his wife strangely. "No, I didn't. Look, if you really want steak, I can go into town and buy some."

Meg ignored him. "Ben didn't eat it and I didn't. So, did you, Laura? Oh, no. I forgot, you don't like red meat, do you?"

"What's this about, Meg?" Ben asked, looking from Meg to Laura. Laura closed the refrigerator door and turned toward them.

Instead of answering, Meg got up and walked to her coat. She reached inside and took out something wrapped in paper.

"While I was waiting for the sheriff to interview me, I had time to think. So many strange things have been happening. And do you know what, Laura? The only connection that I could make between them is that you are always there. I thought about when Bessy nearly died and then what happened in the gallery this morning. All these things have happened since you arrived in our house."

"Meg, I know you're upset, but that's a horrible thing to say," Laura said.

"I went on the motorbike down to the place where I found our dog. Bessy is very good; she won't eat anything unless someone gives her food. And do you know what she likes best of all? Steak. Now who would use steak to give a poor animal poison and then lock her in a building to die?" She stopped and looked into Laura's eyes. "It would need to be someone who really didn't like dogs." As she spoke she opened the paper. Inside was a large piece of steak. "This is what I found when I went to the building where I found Bessy. I'm giving it to the veterinarian to check. It's my guess he'll find poison in it."

"Is this true?" Ben asked, looking at Laura in horror.

Laura laughed and shook her head. "This is crazy. You don't believe her, do you, Ben? She really needs help." She looked from Ben to Meg. "Ben, you can't believe this crazy talk!" She looked at his face as he took a step closer to his wife. "Oh, I see. Well, I don't need to stay here and listen to this. I'm going upstairs to get my things."

Laura came down a little while later, carrying her bag. Meg sat at the table watching her as she walked down the stairs.

"I'm really sorry it ended like this," Laura's voice was no longer confident. She looked very young, like a schoolgirl. "I was so happy to see you again, Meg." She sounded like she was going to cry.

"I still don't understand why you did those things," Meg said.

"I didn't do anything, and it's crazy to say I did. I really think you need help, Meg." Laura turned toward the door. She picked up her bag and paused.

"Oh, I don't have my watch. Have you seen it? It's gold."

Ben looked around impatiently. "Where did you last have it?" he asked.

"Upstairs, I think."

"I'll go and look. Is it in your room?" Ben asked.

"I'm not sure. I'll come and help you look." Laura followed him up.

Meg could hear their voices. Ben came downstairs slowly. He was holding the watch in his hand. Laura followed, her face serious. Meg sat at the kitchen table watching them.

"So, you found it. Where was it?" she asked.

"It was in a box in your closet, Meg." He walked over and stood behind her chair.

Laura looked at her sadly. "Meg, if you needed money you only had to ask. I really think you need help. Don't you agree, Ben?" she said quietly.

"Yes, I do," Ben nodded. Meg looked up at him. He put his hand on her shoulder and continued, "and I think the best help Meg can have is that you leave right now." He threw the watch across the table. "I don't know what game you are playing, Laura, but I trust my wife and I know she's not a thief. She didn't steal Gloria's money and she didn't steal your watch."

"Not a thief?" There was no longer any softness in Laura's voice. "She's the worst thief of all."

"What are you talking about?" Meg stood up, her hands on the table. "Tell me why you did this? What did I ever do to you?"

"You and your stupid club stole the only person that I ever cared about." She took a step forward, eyes glaring. Ben stopped her before she could get to his wife. He pushed her outside and closed the door.

They could still hear her angry voice out in the yard. Her face suddenly appeared on the other side of the window. "You stole from me, Meg," she shouted. "Wait till you lose someone, then you'll know how I feel!"

There was the sound of a car door shutting and an engine starting. They listened as the car drove quickly away. Ben came and put his arms around Meg.

"It's OK, it's all over now," he said quietly. Slowly Meg's breathing started to return to normal.

"Has she really hated me all these years?" she asked.

"Maybe I should phone the sheriff."

Meg thought for a moment then shook her head. "No. It feels horrible to think that I made her hate me so much with that stupid college club of mine. I don't want her to get into trouble. I just want her out of Cornish and out of our life."

"She'll be miles away by now," Ben said later that evening as they got ready for bed. But he checked all the locks two or three times and kept his cell phone nearby.

As she lay in bed, Meg stared into the darkness and wondered if they were wrong not to phone the sheriff and tell him about Laura. But there was no evidence. Why would he believe them? She'll be miles away by now, she repeated Ben's words over and over, but still sleep didn't come.

"I know she's gone, but I can feel her," Meg thought and felt the cold night air against her face.

Chapter 11

A discovery under the bridge

Meg woke and struggled to sit up. Her arms and legs felt heavy. Blue light came though the window. Something had woken her. What was it? Banging. Where was it coming from? She stood and made her way downstairs.

"I'm coming," she called. Above her she could hear the sound of Ben getting out of bed.

She looked though the window and saw the lights of the sheriff's car. She unlocked the door. The sheriff stood in the doorway and took off his hat when he saw her.

"Meg, sorry to trouble you at this time of the morning, but I have some news."

"Come in, Sheriff. What is it?" Ben appeared behind his wife.

"I'm afraid it's your friend, Laura Marsh. We found her car in the river under the covered bridge."

"Oh no, is she hurt?" Meg's hand went to her mouth.

"We haven't found Laura yet, only her car. We don't know if it was an accident or if she wanted to drive in. When did you last see her?"

"At about eight o'clock this evening," Ben said.

"Did she seem upset?"

Meg nodded. "We argued. She was driving back to New York." Her face was pale with shock.

"Do you think she's . . ." Meg couldn't say the word.

"At the moment we're treating her as a missing person. But we have to expect the worst." He looked at her kindly. "Do you know if she has any family?"

Meg shook her head, thinking how little she really knew about Laura.

"No, but she's a writer for *Avant Garde Magazine*. Call them and they'll give you more information."

Meg and Ben walked to the door with the sheriff as he left. "I'll let you know if we have any more news," he promised before getting into his car.

Later that morning, the phone rang making them both jump. It was the sheriff again.

"Meg, are you sure Laura was a writer?" he asked.

"Yes, she was here to interview artists in New Hampshire. Why? What's happened?"

"I contacted the magazine as soon as it opened. They have a Laura Marsh working there, but she's an assistant, not a journalist. She wasn't writing any story. The office says she's supposed to be on vacation at the moment."

Meg shook her head, wondering how many other lies Laura had told her. A sudden thought came to her, filling her with fear.

"Vince, have you heard from Gloria? Laura said she'd gone to stay with her sister, but after what you just told me, I don't know if that's true."

The sheriff was quiet for a moment, thinking.

"I talked to Gloria yesterday and she didn't say anything about going to her sister's place," he said slowly. "In fact, she was supposed to meet me earlier this morning. She had some documents she wanted me to sign about the fire for her insurers."

"What do you mean, she was supposed to meet you?" Meg asked sharply.

"She didn't show up for our appointment. I thought she'd forgotten and tried to call her cell phone, but she didn't answer."

Meg's hand tightened on the phone. "I'm worried. Will you go over to Gloria's place now to check she's OK? I'll meet you there."

"Sure, I'll go right away."

She explained to Ben what had happened and grabbed her coat.

"Wait, I'll get Jack and we'll come with you," he said.

"No, wait here, I'll come straight back. I just need to know that Gloria is OK."

The sheriff's car was already parked outside Gloria's house when Meg arrived. The front door was open and she carefully made her way inside. Gloria's normally neat home was a mess. Chairs and tables were knocked over.

She heard voices from the bedroom and went in. With a cry of relief she saw Gloria sitting up in bed. The doctor was on one side and the sheriff on the other. Gloria was pale, but she smiled and held out her hand when she saw Meg.

"Oh, Gloria, are you OK? What happened?" Meg sat on the bed and took the older woman's hands.

"Well, a night locked in the cellar isn't my idea of fun, but it could have been a lot worse."

"What's the last thing you remember before she hit you?" the sheriff asked.

"Laura came here with Jack. He was playing with his train on the floor. I was still in shock about the fire. Laura was talking about Meg, saying she was ill and needed help. She said Meg had stolen something from her at college. She wasn't making any sense. Then she said it's easy to start a fire with an electric heater and that Meg had probably been trying to burn down the gallery so that I wouldn't find out about the money."

"That's not true!" Meg cried.

"I know that, Meg! That's when I realized. I mean, Laura said she hadn't been in the office that day. So how did she know it was an electric heater? I wanted an excuse to get away from her. So I said we should take Jack to the restaurant to get him something to eat. Next thing, I felt something hit me on the back of my head. When I woke up I was in the dark with my hands and feet tied. Later, I heard Ben's voice when he came to collect Jack, but I couldn't make enough noise for him to hear me."

Meg shook her head. "I still don't understand why she did this. I guess we'll never know now."

"Why? What happened?" Gloria asked.

Meg exchanged glances with the sheriff. "They found Laura's car in the river at five o'clock this morning. We think she could be dead," she said.

"No, Laura's as alive as you or me." Gloria shook her head, pressing her lips together.

"Why do you say that?" the sheriff asked quickly.

"Because I heard her moving about in this house at seven o'clock this morning. Two hours after you found the car in the river. I know it was seven because I heard the church bells ring. I could hear her looking for something. I was really scared; I thought she'd come back to kill me. I didn't hear another thing till the sheriff came here and rescued me."

"You have Meg to thank for that," the sheriff replied. "What do you think she was looking for?"

The question was answered by a young man in uniform. He put his head around the door.

"Sorry to interrupt you, sir, but we've found a purse with five credit cards. One of the credit cards is in the name of Laura Marsh. The other four have different names on them. I checked and they're all stolen."

"Good work," nodded the sheriff. "Anything else?"

"Yes." The young man looked at Gloria. "Sorry, ma'am, but it looks like she stole your car."

"She's taken my car!" Bright spots of anger lit Gloria's face, and she tried to get out of bed.

"Stay there. I haven't finished with you yet," ordered the doctor.

"I don't understand. Do you think Laura had an accident in her car and took Gloria's car to get away?" Meg asked the sheriff.

"No, I think it was all part of her plan. Laura wanted us to think she was dead. While everyone searched for her in the river, she was free to go wherever she wanted. She came back here and took Gloria's car so she can drive around here without anyone noticing her."

"What? You really think she's still in Cornish?" Gloria sounded worried.

"I sure do. If she wanted to leave the area she could be hundreds of miles away by now in her fancy sports car. She wouldn't need your car at all. So now the question is: What unfinished business does Laura have in this town? Where will she go next?"

Meg stood up. "I have to warn Ben. If Gloria has any unfinished business, then it's with me and my family." Fear spread through her as she took out her cell phone. She listened as it rang six, seven times. At last it was picked up.

"Ben," she said quickly, "Laura wasn't in the car that went into the river. Keep the doors locked and don't let Jack out of your sight. I don't think she's finished with us yet."

There was silence at the other end of the phone followed by a low laugh. "No, I haven't finished with you yet, Meg. Remember what I said to you?" Laura's voice was soft. "You stole from me. Well, now I'm stealing from you."

The line went dead.

Chapter 12

Taken

They found Ben in the kitchen, lying across the table. Meg saw the blood and with a cry ran to him. He was still breathing. Her face white, Meg stood and looked around the room.

"Where's Jack?" she asked. "Where's my baby?"

She ran through the house, calling Jack's name. She knew he wasn't there; she could feel that he had been taken. But she needed to check, hoping all the time that she was wrong. When she got back downstairs, the ambulance was there. Two men were lifting Ben into it. She ran to him and kissed his hand.

"I'm going to find Jack, and then I'll be by your side," she said, touching his face.

Pushing past the sheriff, she ran to the truck. The dog followed. "Come on, Bessy, get in," she said.

The sheriff turned at the sound of the engine. "Stop!" He banged on the door. "Where are you going?"

Meg ignored him and looked straight ahead as she drove faster and faster along the track.

Stay calm, she told herself. She tried to imagine the route that Laura would take. The rain had started again, making it almost impossible to see though the car window.

She drove over the covered bridge. As she got to the other side, her cell phone rang. She glanced at it, wondering if it was the sheriff. After a moment's hesitation she reached into her pocket and answered it.

"Mommy, rain." At the sound of her son's voice she almost lost control of the car.

"Hi, Meg." This time it was Laura's voice. She could still hear Jack in the background; he was making train noises.

"Where is my son?" she demanded.

"It's not good to lose someone you love, is it? What does it feel like to have someone steal them away?"

Meg could hardly hear the other woman's voice over the rain drumming on the car roof.

"Let me see Jack," she tried to keep the anger from her voice.

"First I want you to try remembering, Meg. For example, what do you remember about me?"

She listened to Laura's breathing. What else could she hear? Was that the river in the background?

"I'm waiting," Laura's voice was impatient.

"Laura, I'm very sorry I upset you." Meg listened carefully. Yes, that was the river she could hear. But the car, she couldn't hear the car. They must have stopped. Carefully she turned the truck around. After a few hundred yards she turned right onto the river road.

"You can't remember anything about me, can you?" Laura shouted. "When we looked at those old photographs in the college yearbook, you couldn't even recognize me. That's because at college you never looked at me. I was never cool enough for you. You and your friends walked around college like you owned the place, laughing and having your parties that I was never invited to."

She won't hurt Jack, Meg thought. She saved him in the lake. Then she remembered the toy rabbit on the edge of the lake. The toy rabbit that Jack never took out of the house. She imagined Laura looking into the room and finding Jack awake. Laura using the toy as a game to lead him down to the lake and watching while he fell in.

"But your stupid group didn't matter to me. Instead I spent all my time with Doug Martin. We wrote songs together for his band." Laura sounded as though she was talking to herself. "He didn't know that I loved him, but I knew in time he'd feel the same way about me. All I had to do was wait."

There was a sound on the phone. It was difficult to tell if it was crying or the wind in the trees. There was a pause, then Laura spoke again.

"But then you invited him to join your stupid club. It was after a concert his band gave. I watched you come up and talk to him. I remember the look on his face, like he had won a million dollars. After that, I hardly saw him. So I asked if I could join the club, too. But before I could join I had to do a special test, like all the other new members. Do you remember what the test was called?"

Meg felt herself grow cold. "Face your fear," she said quietly. She had almost forgotten; it was such a long time ago. Surely, it had just been a bit of fun. No one took it seriously.

But another picture suddenly came to her of a much younger Laura looking nervous and trying to smile in a room with some of the club members on the day that she did her test.

"And what was I afraid of, Meg? What was the fear you decided I had to face?"

Meg swallowed. "Doug told us you were afraid of dogs."

"That's right. You were the one that told me to sit down and then you covered my eyes. I felt sick with fear, but I would have done anything to be with Doug. I just wanted him to notice me again. Suddenly I heard the most terrifying noise. It sounded like the room was filled with dogs, ready to bite me."

With shame Meg remembered Laura running from the room, screaming, eyes wide with fear.

"You were all laughing at me." There was no emotion in Laura's voice; it was empty. "Of course, I failed the test so I never did join the club. You sat next to me in a class a few days later and you didn't even recognize me. Then you and Doug started dating. He had no interest in me after that. He was the only person I wanted, and you took him. It doesn't feel good to lose someone, Meg, does it?"

"Laura, I'm truly sorry, please believe me."

There was the sound of distant, breathless voices. Laura hadn't turned off her phone. Meg heard the sound of someone falling and a cry—Jack's cry.

"Laura," she called into her cell phone. But there was no answer.

"Be quiet!" she heard Laura yell to Jack. "Leave it! It's too heavy."

Meg drove faster. She turned a corner and saw a tree. It had fallen across the road. She tried to stop, but it was too late. Instead she turned to the left. The truck went onto the grass. Branches hit the roof and doors. The truck shook. Meg thought it was going to fall into the river. Then suddenly it came to a stop. She sat for a moment, her hands shaking. Then she got out of the truck and opened the back door. The dog jumped out.

Suddenly she saw something large and black at the side of the road. It was shining in the rain. Her heart started to beat faster. She realized that she was looking at Gloria's stolen car.

Chapter 13

The water's edge

Meg ran to the car and opened the door. It was empty. She took her cell phone from her pocket. She could still hear Laura speaking. In the background, the river was louder now. She turned and ran through the trees toward the water. As she ran, she saw something red on the ground. It was Jack's train.

At the water's edge she looked right and left. Brushing rain from her face, she walked along the river. Behind her, in the distance, she could see the covered bridge. It was hard to believe that her home was only a few miles away, warm and dry and safe. She wanted to sit down and cry. The dog ran ahead. She took a deep breath and followed.

She heard Laura before she saw her.

"Get the dog away," Laura was shouting angrily.

Meg ran in the direction of the voice. Laura stood on the edge of the water, near a small boat. She held Jack with one arm. He was crying. When he saw Meg he put his arms out toward her. But Laura wouldn't let him go.

"Give me Jack," Meg said quietly. The other woman ignored her. With her free hand, Laura tried to grab the boat. It was old and there was water in it.

"Laura, that boat is dangerous. Don't try to get in," Meg warned.

"Don't tell me what to do." Laura's hair was wet. "Do you know how I found you? I was working as an assistant at

Avant Garde Magazine. Last month I was filing information about new artists. I dropped a brochure about Gloria's gallery, and when I picked it up, there was your face staring out at me across the years. Instead of filing it, I took it home to my tiny apartment. Every night I looked at it and read about your perfect life in the country with your husband and son. That's the life I should have had with Doug, the life you stole from me."

"Nobody's life is perfect," Meg shouted into the wind. "You've seen that I have problems just like you, just like everyone. Laura, I am truly sorry that I hurt you at college. The tests were a horrible thing to do, and the club was stupid. But I was young. I'm not the same person as I was then."

But Laura wasn't listening. "You didn't even care about Doug, did you? After a month you left him for someone else. I thought he'd come back to me then, but he didn't. He just followed you around like a little puppy dog hoping you would talk to him. I don't suppose you noticed that either, did you?"

"We were kids," Meg said. She started to walk slowly toward Jack.

"I loved seeing the envy in your eyes when you saw my clothes and car. I could see it in your eyes. Imagine that! College queen Meg Sears wanted to be boring little Laura Marsh," she laughed, then her expression hardened. "I thought, you took Doug, so I'll take your husband. But he wasn't interested. All he wanted to talk about was you." She was crying now, hot angry tears.

"We could have been friends," Meg said. "Remember the day we went shopping in Cornish together?" She looked at her son's frightened face. "We could still be friends. Just give me Jack."

Laura looked at Meg. She was like a person waking after a long sleep.

"I don't want to be your friend. I want to steal from you like you stole from me. This time I'll make sure that you don't forget me," she shouted.

Meg leaned forward to take Jack. Laura tried to hold him. Suddenly, the dog jumped up. Laura cried out and took a step back, letting go of Jack. Meg got him and held him in her arms. With a scream, Laura fell backwards. She tried to grab a branch, but it broke. Meg reached out her hand but was too late. Laura continued falling, over the edge and into the river.

There was a shout, and Meg turned to see the sheriff running toward her. She ran to him and gently put Jack in his arms. Then she hurried back to the river and climbed into the small boat.

The sheriff was speaking into his radio as Meg pushed the boat out into the river. The water was flowing fast toward the bridge. She struggled to control the boat as the river pulled it along. Laura was holding on to a branch. Meg leaned over and held out her hand. Laura hesitated, then reached out to take it. But just as their fingers touched, the wind got stronger, taking the boat farther into the center of the river. Meg watched in horror as Laura's other hand slipped off the branch. She tried to swim, but her head disappeared under the water. She rose up once, coughing. But then the river carried her away, and the water closed over her head. With the last of her strength, Meg turned the boat. The sheriff was waiting for her. He reached down, helping her onto the grass. In the distance, Meg could hear a police car getting closer.

Chapter 14

The first snow of winter

A month after Laura's body was found under the covered bridge, the first snow came. Meg walked with Gloria across the white fields at the back of the farm. The dog ran ahead, smelling a rabbit. Jack was up ahead with his father. He jumped happily in his new snow boots and threw snow at Ben. Meg smiled at her husband. The scar on his head had almost gone. They often talked about what had happened that day. The distance between them had gone.

Ben picked up his son and put him on his shoulders. They walked ahead calling the dog to come and play.

Gloria waited until they had disappeared into the woodland. Then she turned to Meg.

"So, how are things?" she asked quietly.

"Good," Meg replied. "After what happened we realized that there are worse things than worrying about a new roof for the house." She tried to smile, but the memory of the fast-flowing river still gave her nightmares. They followed the path down toward the lake.

"It meant a lot to me that you and Ben never believed I took that money," Meg said at last.

"You've got to trust the people you love. Otherwise, what's the point?" Gloria answered.

"Yes, I think I finally understand that." Meg looked over at her husband playing in the snow with their son.

She thought about Laura and the unhappiness she had carried with her for so long. "Laura came here because of what I did at college. She had all that hate in her for so long because of the way I made her feel," Meg said.

"Meg, you were just young. You didn't think . . ."

"But that's just it, Gloria, I didn't think. To me it was all just fun and games. I didn't think about how it feels not to belong, not to be part of the group."

Gloria put her hand on Meg's arm. "You're not responsible for what Laura did. We all have choices."

They walked in silence for a moment, looking at the white trees.

"I'm glad you decided to stay in Cornish. I was worried that you might leave," Gloria said.

"This is our home." Meg looked at the lake, hills, and fields. And she realized that it was true. It was her family home. With a little work, they could be happy here.

Ben and Jack walked back to the two women. The dog jumped beside them, leaving prints in the snow.

"Come on, Jack. Let's race Mom and Dad back to the house." Gloria lifted him down from Ben's shoulders. "Last one back doesn't get any chocolate cake."

Ben took Meg's hand, and they turned and walked toward the house together.

Review: Chapters 1—5

A. Match the name to the description.

1. Meg   **a.** works with computers.

2. Jack   **b.** owns an art gallery.

3. Gloria   **c.** lives in New York.

4. Ben   **d.** is an artist.

5. Laura   **e.** is a dog.

6. Doug   **f.** is two years old.

7. Bessy   **g.** is Meg's old boyfriend.

B. Choose the best answer for each question.

1. Where did Meg and Laura first meet?

    a. a party   b. college   c. work

2. Why is Laura in town?

    a. to buy paintings   b. to visit old friends   c. to interview artists

3. Why is Laura staying with Meg and Ben?

    a. She has a problem with her car.

    b. She lost her purse.

    c. She has an appointment in town.

4. What is Ben worried about?

    a. his son   b. money   c. his car

5. Meg was worried because . . .

    a. Laura wanted to stay in a hotel.

    b. Ben burned the dinner.

    c. Laura and Ben were late getting back.

C. Read each statement and circle whether it is true (T) or false (F).

At college:

1. Meg and Laura were best friends.   T / F
2. Laura was in Meg's club.   T / F
3. Meg was popular.   T / F
4. Laura was quiet.   T / F
5. They both knew Doug.   T / F

D. Complete the crossword puzzle using the clues below.

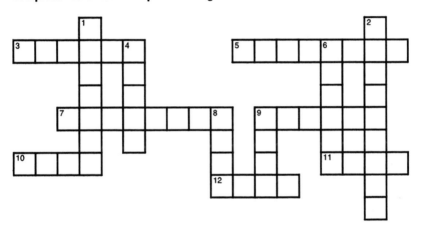

Across

3. the musical instrument Doug played
5. Meg and Laura go _____ in town.
7. Laura phoned the _____ about her car.
9. Laura helps cook the _____.
10. Laura doesn't eat red _____.
11. Ben wears a _____ for his meeting with the bank
12. Ben used to go to lunch with his _____.

Down

1. Laura was a _____ at Dover College.
2. *Avant Garde Magazine* wants to _____ Meg.
4. Meg tells Ben they did the _____ thing moving from New York to New Hampshire.
6. Meg _____ pictures in her studio.
8. At college Meg started her own _____.
9. Laura is afraid of these.

Review: Chapters 6–10

A. Number these events in the order that they happened.

a. There is a fire at the gallery. _____

b. Laura leaves. _____

c. The dog goes missing. _____

d. The sheriff questions Meg. _____

e. Jack goes missing. _____

f. The mechanic fixes the car. _____

g. Ben finds Laura's watch. _____

h. Laura saves Jack from the lake. _____

i. They go to a restaurant. _____

j. Jack breaks the glass statues. _____

B. Read each statement and circle whether it is true (T) or false (F).

1. Ben thinks that Meg doesn't trust him. T / F

2. Laura plans to spend her vacation in Miami. T / F

3. Meg can ride a motorbike. T / F

4. The fire starts in Gloria's office. T / F

5. The gallery is destroyed by the fire. T / F

6. Ben believes that Meg steals things. T / F

7. Meg thinks that Laura used the steak to poison the dog. T / F

C. Match each question with the correct answer.

Who . . .

1. advises Laura to take her car to a garage in New York?

2. asks if any of the farms uses rat poison?

3. carries equipment in the art gallery?

4. finds two thousand dollars in a desk?

a. the veterinarian

b. the mechanic

c. the sheriff

d. the firefighters

D. Choose the best answer for each question.

1. When Meg says to Ben, "Well it seems you made her so welcome she wants to stay" on page 40, what is she referring to?

   a. that she is worried that Ben is attracted to Laura

   b. that Ben invited Laura to stay

   c. that Gloria is attracted to Ben

2. What does Meg mean when she asks, "Gloria, did you forget to go to the bank again" on page 48?

   a. that this is the first time that Gloria forgot to go to the bank

   b. that Gloria often forgets to go to the bank

   c. that Gloria forgot to give her some money

3. When Laura says, "She's the worst thief of all" on page 65, she is saying that Meg stole . . .

   a. a car Laura owned.

   b. a person Laura cared about.

   c. Laura's place in a club.

Review: Chapters 11–14

A. Complete the crossword puzzle using the clues below.

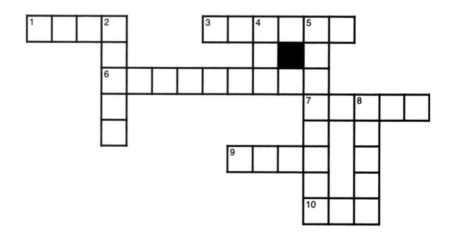

Across

1. Meg uses a(n) _____ to try to help Laura in the river.

3. Laura says that Gloria has gone to stay with her _____.

6. Ben went to the hospital in a(n) _____.

7. Laura pays for things using stolen credit _____.

9. The club test was called "Face Your _____."

10. Laura stole Gloria's _____.

Down

2. Meg finds a toy _____.

4. Jack is Meg's _____.

5. Laura used a(n) _____ heater to start the fire.

8. Laura's car is found in the _____.

B. Read each statement and circle whether it is true (T) or false (F).

1. Meg is the first to arrive at Gloria's house. T / F

2. Laura hit Gloria on the head. T / F

3. Gloria heard Laura at seven o'clock at night. T / F

4. Laura used stolen credit cards. T / F

5. Gloria has a sister. T / F

6. Laura swims to safety. T / F

7. Laura was in love with Doug. T / F

8. Meg and Ben move back to New York. T / F

C. Complete the summary below by using the words in the box.

guilty	life	trust	college
save	friend	love	

Laura was in **1.** _____ with a boy when she was in **2.** _____. She thinks
that Meg stole him from her. She pretends to be Meg's **3.** _____ but she
wants to destroy Meg's **4.** _____. Meg feels **5.** _____ for the way she
treated Laura at college. Laura falls into the river and Meg tries to
6. _____ her. At the end of the story, Meg realizes that it is important to
7. _____ the people she loves.

Answer Key

Chapters 1–5

A:

1. d; **2.** f; **3.** b; **4.** a; **5.** c; **6.** g; **7.** e

B:

1. b; **2.** c; **3.** a; **4.** b; **5.** c

C:

1. F; **2.** T; **3.** F; **4.** T; **5.** T

D:

Across:

3. guitar; **5.** shopping; **7.** mechanic; **9.** dinner; **10.** meat; **11.** suit; **12.** boss

Down:

1. student; **2.** interview; **4.** right; **6.** paints; **8.** club; **9.** dogs

Chapters 6–10

A:

In order: i, e, h, f, c, j, a, d, g, b

B:

1. T; **2.** F; **3.** T; **4.** T; **5.** F; **6.** F; **7.** T

C:

1. b; **2.** a; **3.** d; **4.** c

D:

1. a; **2.** b; **3.** b

Chapters 11–14

A:

Across:

1. boat; **3.** sister; **6.** ambulance; **7.** cards; **9.** fear; **10.** car

Down:

2. train; **4.** son; **5.** electric; **8.** river

B:

1. F; **2.** T; **3.** F; **4.** T; **5.** T; **6.** F; **7.** T; **8.** F

C:

1. love; **2.** college; **3.** friend; **4.** life; **5.** guilty; **6.** save; **7.** trust

Background Reading:

Spotlight on ... *Reunions*

There are more than 150,000 college and high school reunions in the USA every year. A reunion is an organized event to get together people who went to the same school or college. It seems like a great idea: you can visit your old school or college and discover what old friends have been doing. But not everyone likes going to a reunion. In a recent survey only 22% of people said that they were happy when they thought about reunions. One of the reasons is that a college reunion makes you think about your own life and what you have done since you left school or college. Suddenly you need to compare your job, financial success, and attractiveness with people that you haven't seen for years. So what is likely to make someone decide to go to a reunion? A special date is important; for example, more people will attend a reunion to celebrate ten years since they left college than a reunion after six or seven years. People are also more likely to go if they think they are a success; only 20% of those who earn less than $30,000 said that they would attend a reunion compared with more than 60% of those that earn more than $50,000.

Look at the words below. Which ones describe how you would feel about going to a school or college reunion? Can you add any other words that you might feel?

- happy
- excited
- uncomfortable
- worried
- interested
- angry
- pleased
- proud
- anxious

Glossary

assistant	(*n.*)	an office worker who helps another
barn	(*n.*)	a farm building
brochure	(*n.*)	a short booklet that contains information or advertising
cellar	(*n.*)	a room under a house
classmate	(*n.*)	someone in the same class at school or college
closet	(*n.*)	a room for clothes
flashlight	(*n.*)	a light you can carry
gallery	(*n.*)	a place to look at and buy art
gossip	(*v.*)	to chat about people
puppy dog	(*n.*)	baby dog
scar	(*n.*)	a mark left from a wound
sheriff	(*n.*)	person who keeps law and order in a county
stove	(*n.*)	an appliance to cook food on or in
studio	(*n.*)	a room where an artist can paint
thief	(*n.*)	someone who steals
track	(*n.*)	small and rough road
veterinarian	(*n.*)	a doctor for animals